ANTHOLOGY OF SERBIA

ANTHOLOGY OF SERBIA

1st Edition : APRIL 2023
Published by Cooch Behar
Copyright © 2023 **ANTHOLOGY OF SERBIA**

All rights reserved.
ISBN: 9798393012588
PUBLISHED FROM
COOCH BEHAR CITY
INDIA
Order books from Amazon.com

DEDICATION

Poets of Serbia

ANTHOLOGY OF SERBIA

Editor : SOURAV SARKAR
Copyright © 2023 **ANTHOLOGY OF SERBIA**

ISBN: 9798393012588

©ALL RIGHTS RESERVED
No part of this book may be reproduced, stored in a retrieval system, or transmitted in any form or by any means, electronic, mechanical, photocopying, recording or otherwise, without the prior written permission of the author.

Published –29APRIL2023

PREFACE

Serbia is a country of great writers.
Editor
ANTHOLOGY OF SERBIA
SOURAV SARKAR

ANTHOLOGY OF SERBIA

List of Poets
Follow Serial Numbers To read Poems

1) Milana Janjičić
2) Mladomir Knežević
3) Verica Tadić
4) Viktor Radun Teon
5) Vera Cvetanović
6) Nedeljko Terzić
7) Ivana Milankov
8) IOAN BABA

TO THE DECEASED
Milana Janjičić

It's not her anymore.
He will not be resurrected.
She shook herself
futility and hope.
She got lost in the maze
memory,
the memories flooded back
her being.
Covered with a veil of small things
pieces of sadness,
be in vain.
She died last night.

Mladomir Knežević

For her

Perfection in love
to prepare skillfully
And it is always at the meeting
around my heart burning
He would like to make love with
her
impossible to resist
A challenge, it's cute
I burn in the fire of love
Cuvik of real feelings
multiplies instantly
She is worthy of love
to the heart, to the soul, that is
clear
Eh,how it turns me on
a strong fire in the chest
I dream the moment of the
event
both during the day and after
dark
Constantly in my mind
it's mine, he walks with them
It is a source of inspiration
the love in my soul is strong for
her.

Verica Tadić

LA FORTUNE

Two halves

Have been searching

For each other

For centuries

They are attracted

By the same smell

They recognize

Themselves by it

If they

Find each other

Stars will dance

On the blue trapeze

Angels will walk

On toes through

The harmony

On

The wedding cake

New Moon

Will write

down the date.

Viktor Radun Teon
Fading of a poem

Viktor Radun Teon
Novi Sad, Serbia

I break an Aquamarine
into four slices
watching the reflection
wither away
a poem fading
by open pane
the Elements dying
therein

Viktor Radun Teon
On my palm

As the blue of morning is
prying on
maddened birds
from every crevice
wild shadows
crawl
amid a desolate Agora
amongst the stifled words
rises Atlantis
I rediscover you
the primal jasmine
blossoming on my palm
Close the door
come closer
there' s a storm outside
Here' s an oyster
here am I

THE MELODY OF INEXPRESSIBLE

Vera Cvetanović

There is something of fairy kind in these areas,

Unreal shades radiate endlessly,

Coloured by angelic emeralds

With stunning glamour of constant faith.

I love those mystical spheres

I wish I could stay here longer

My cheerful heart absorbs the joy,

I celebrate the gold crown and the brooch

The shadow of a pilgrim stretches far

Where the prayer hums in its waves

The pilgrim carries it deep in his heart

The prayer whispers the message of love and peace

It weaves silver threads

The melody of inexpressible pulsates quietly.

Nedeljko Terzić

DOMESTIC SONG

There I am.

Watching through the window.

And I see myself walking along a road.

The road is like broken glass.

I know everything as if I had seen.

There I am, at your home.

Walking on broken glass.

The places are known to me,

the seed of plants I'm walking on

is known to me,

and you are also konwn to me.

And there I am, on the far away road.

I'm swinging from the exclamation mark

to the question mark:

I'm alive brother!

There I go.

It's time for me.

FATHER STEPS FORWARD

They predicted that my blood

Would become black water.

In my thirtieth

I'd watch into the roots of grass.

They would dress me a wooden suit.

They cursed me for thousand times.

They attackend me only to see

how would I defend myself.

I survived.

Their blood became black river.

In their thirtieth

they watched into the roots of grass.

Wooden suits were made for them.

I've never cursed them.

Your father knows where he is going to.

CRETAN SISTERS

Ivana Milankov

My Cretan sisters

I am waiting for you

to change from lava into lighting,

your volcanoes,

snakes and earthshaking goddesses

to slough your skin

and to dream a pure deram in water.

I am waiting for you

and becoming the Danube,

In the spring minds of lightning

so as to escort you.

IOAN BABA

IT'S DEFINITELY TRUE – VICE VERSA

The poet hardens his words like a blacksmith

Who exclusively shoes

Those who cannot shoe themselves

The bizarre question is

Does the Horseshoer-Poet

Shoe himself or not

If he shoes himself

It results he doesn't belong

To the horseherd of those who don't have to be shoed

Since he doesn't shoe

Then he belongs

ANTHOLOGY OF SERBIA

To the crowd

Made of those who don't shoe themselves

And then what am I

Who harden my poems myself

Between Sense and Nonsense

What a strange proposition

When uttering now this

Now the other

I lie and I don't lie in the least

So why should I vainly

Queue

To be shoed

English version by GABRIELA PACHIA

ANTHOLOGY OF SERBIA

ANTHOLOGY OF SERBIA

ANTHOLOGY OF SERBIA

ANTHOLOGY OF SERBIA

Printed in Great Britain
by Amazon